D0918975

My First Animal Library

Gorillas

by Mari Schuh

Bullfrog Books

Ideas for Parents and Teachers

Bullfrog Books give children practice reading informational text at the earliest levels. Repetition, familiar words, and photos support early readers.

Before Reading

• Discuss the cover photo. What does it tell them?

• Look at the picture glossary together. Read and discuss the words.

Read the Book

• "Walk" through the book and look at the photos. Let the child ask questions. Point out the photo labels.

• Read the book to the child, or have him or her read independently.

After Reading

• Prompt the child to think more. Ask: How is a gorilla troop like your family? Do you groom each other? Do you nap together?

Dedicated to the Martin County Library—MS

Bullfrog Books are published by Jump!
5357 Penn Avenue South
Minneapolis, MN 55419
www.jumplibrary.com

Library of Congress Cataloging-in-Publication Data
Schuh, Mari C., 1975- author.
  Gorillas / by Mari Schuh.
    pages cm. —(My first animal library)
  Summary: "This photo-illustrated book for early readers tells the story of a troop of gorillas spending the day in the rain forest"—Provided by publisher.
  Audience: 5-8.
  Audience: Grade K to 3.
  Includes bibliographical references and index.
  ISBN 978-1-62031-109-7 (hardcover)
  ISBN 978-1-62496-176-2 (ebook)
  1. Gorilla—Juvenile literature. I. Title.
  QL737.P96S38 2015
  599.884--dc23
                              2013042374

Editor: Wendy Dieker
Series Designer: Ellen Huber
Book Designer: Lindaanne Donohoe
Photo Researcher: Kurtis Kinneman

Photo Credits: All photos by Shutterstock except Alamy 5, 6-7, 10, 18-19, 20-21; Corbis 13; Superstock 14-15, 17, 23, 24;

Printed in the United States of America at Corporate Graphics, North Mankato, Minnesota.
6-2014
10 9 8 7 6 5 4 3 2 1

Table of Contents

Life in a Troop

A new day is here.
Gorillas wake up.

Gorillas live
in a troop.

It is their family.

silver
hair

An older male
is the leader.

He is a silverback.

The hair on his
back is silver.

The troop looks for food.
They walk in the rain forest.

Babies get a ride.
Thanks, Mom!

Look!
They find fruit.
They eat leaves
and bark, too.
They eat all day.

berries

It's time to rest.
They groom each other.
Yawn!
They nap, too.

**Oh no!
A leopard!**

The silverback beats his chest.
Thump! Thump!

Roar!

Look at his big teeth.

The leopard runs away.

The troop is safe.

Night is coming.
The gorillas make nests.
Now they go to sleep.
Good night!

Parts of a Gorilla

forehead
A gorilla's big forehead protects its small eyes.

arm
A gorilla's arms are longer than its legs.

feet
Gorillas use their feet to hold onto things, just like hands.

Picture Glossary

groom
To take care
of and to clean.

silverback
An adult male
gorilla.

rain forest
A thick area
of trees where
a lot of rain falls.

troop
A group of
gorillas that
live together.

Index

To Learn More

Learning more is as easy as 1, 2, 3.

1) Go to www.factsurfer.com

2) Enter "gorillas" into the search box.

3) Click the "Surf" button to see a list of websites.

With factsurfer.com, finding more information is just a click away.